Beautiful Mind is Everything in Life

Muhammad Abdal

ISBN: 9798848402247

DEDICATION

I dedicate this book to all of my teachers who provided me best possible support and guidance especially when I needed it most. It's honour for me to mention that my teachers are my pride. Moreover, my family members especially my father supported me, and it is mean to me and I will commemorate his support for all of my life.

CONTENTS

ACKNOWLEDGMENTS

I would like to thank my teachers and my family members who encouraged me to write. I would like to thank Tutor Ones Zaidi from Tunis, Mr. Shahid Naz, Mr. Rizwan, Mr. Talat, Mrs. Aneela and Mrs. Sadia from Pakistan. At the end, I you like to thank YOU for taking time to read this book. I wish you all the best in your life.

The significance of creativity in study

A lot of people believe that creativity comes naturally. There's some creative spark inside us that can't be taught; it just shows up when you least expect it. I would say "creativity" is too broad a term to define a skill set. But the truth is, creativity comes from a well of inner energy. If you are creative, chances are you have an innate sense of what works and what doesn't.

That's why the process of getting through graduate school involves an unending stream of creativity, innovation, and invention. This is one of the things that separate graduate school from college. In graduate school, you're forced to think outside the box. For example, in college, you can do a project in which you repeat what someone else has already said in a new way. But when working on your thesis or dissertation, you may need to reinvent the wheel from scratch.

The Power of Book Reading for Creativity

There are many ways you can become more creative. One of those ways is through the power of book reading. Just think about it. You can read books by people who were born in another century. You can read books by writers you've never heard of. And you can read books by people who did things you would never consider doing. Look at all the books about travel, adventure, business, and sports. You can learn from people who faced challenging situations and survived and those who did incredible things and didn't even know it!

Reading books is proven to stimulate your brain and improve your ability to problem-solve. It's also proven to increase your creativity. You can apply for those proven benefits in all areas of your life, including creativity, problem-solving, innovation, and leadership.

Read one book every day, and you'll never get stuck again. The power of reading is the power of inspiration. And you don't need to read a lot. Just read one good book daily, and you'll never get stuck again.

What Can You Do to Create Amazing Paintings For Creativity

Creativity doesn't just happen. It would help if you put in a lot of hard work. It takes patience. A lot of practice. But don't worry. There is always a way to learn the tricks of the trade, and today we're going to show you a straightforward method to help you achieve great artistic results.

There's a simple way to use colour to get creative: Play with colour. That's all. You'll notice that many of the most successful artists have one thing in common: They use colour to express their ideas. Colour is a powerful medium of expression. So what can you do to use colour to express yourself? Just follow these tips:

1. Colour can inspire. Look at the colours of nature and the colours of the objects you surround yourself with.
2. Choose colours that work well together. You'll see they work together if you see a red hat, green shirt, and blue pants.
3. Mix primary and secondary colours.

Diary Writing – Why Do People Keep Diaries

In the past, diaries were used for several purposes. They were kept as personal journals and records of important events in a person's life. They could also be used as a form of self-help. By recording the thoughts and feelings of an individual, the individual could learn to deal with any difficult situation or emotional problem that came his or her way.

Currently, most people keep diaries, but there are different reasons why they might keep one. Here are the most common reasons people write in their diaries: To document significant moments in our lives. To remember things we think we will forget. To share with others the things that have happened to us. And keep track of all the things we need to remember.

Best possible outcome if we develop creativity

When we start exploring the concept of creativity, we begin to see that we can create anything we want. And that is true. But that also means we have more freedom than we've ever had before. We will have a solid foundation for our future. If we don't have much money, we will still make the most of our creativity.

Best Tips for Being Productive

Among all other activities of daily routine, studying makes you a better person. Here, in this article, you will read about the best tips to be productive during the study. It is not just a matter of studying; it covers all spheres of life. You have to be straightforward regarding your plans or schedules. Being irresponsible and irregular in doing different things creates several problems for you. Therefore, here are some special tips and advice for getting most of your reading activity.

Here are some of the best tips for becoming productive in your study. You have to be focused when following a schedule or timetable for studying different stuff. It is always helpful in producing excellent results.

Study when you have no worries!

This thing is of immense importance in the activity of reading. Most critiques and writers recommend it for you. You have their suggestions in front to act accordingly. It is admitted that worries would never put you in peace and comfort of mind. It will keep you from achieving good results whenever you switch to this great activity. Never pick up a book when you are worried or depressed due to any reason.

Following a set timetable

It is very important and special in the case of studying. Regularity and punctuality bring forth amazing outputs in life. The first thing that matters when studying is following your already planned timetable. If you follow this schedule, studying will become an easy go for you! The status of your serene inner environment becomes ideal for you.

Develop a love of studying in yourself

This element must be ranked at the top of the list. Eagerness and interest in the activity of studying matter a lot. Without these two elements, you cannot complete your objectives. You must be a good reader. You need to increase your love of learning and study literature yourself. These things are clear identification of your seriousness about studying.

Getting rid of negative and destructive thoughts

It is always important in the activity of studying. You must always be humble and positive all the time. It is really important to be productive by studying different subjects. To achieve ideal results, you must keep negative and destructive thoughts at arm's length to have a good command over your study approach. Your unwanted thoughts are a big threat to your set plans.

Keep a good focus and concentration.

Focus and concentration on studying different stuff and pieces of literature matter a lot. You can't keep your concentration and target off when your eagerness touches the sky. You need to get yourself engaged in this activity. Without concentration on your studying, you cannot be perfect and productive in your study because everything is done for a certain purpose.

Have a clear objective!

Your target or objective must be confirmed and crystal clear before you get to the task. Without having a clear objective, you cannot shape your future destination. Becoming a better citizen should be a part of your goal. It must be confirmed. Your objectives in studying help you a lot to get along with your bright career. Apart from that, your set objective defines who you are and what you want.

Reserve a good portion of your time for other activities.

Remember, guys, never become a bookworm in your life! Keep your activity of studying and your personal life apart. Excess to everything is always bad. It is never welcomed at any level. You need to engage in other activities with some free time from studying books or other literature items. These activities may include walking, playing badminton, football, or cricket. You can also find new folks and friends. It will keep your mental health in good shape.

Get some time for a walk.

Getting some time for a walk and having an outing in vacant time produce wonderful outputs. This amazing thing will leave pleasing effects on your life. The imprints of what you last studied refresh your memory. You need to do it to keep you vibrant all the time. This way, your studying will always be beneficial and productive for you.

Find some time for the world!

This segment of this process is very important. You must

socialize your life. It gives rise to your observations received from studying. Therefore, never cut yourself off from the people around you! They are a source of motivation and living experiences for you.

Read the best stuff!

This thing never gets more important than how much you study. The actual thing that matters is what you study. Your selection of books or other literature items must be nice and wise. A healthy reading is real reading!

Conclusion

In short, studying different stuff is a powerful source to adorn your personal life. The study leaves an amazing effect on your personality. Studying helps in shaping your personality! The study will make your life productive, not only for you but also for others around!

Development Of Memory for Study

What is The Significance of Creativity in Study

Creativity is the ability to generate new ideas or solutions to problems. Creativity is thinking outside the box and seeing possibilities that others miss. Creativity is what makes you different from everyone else. So, you need to learn to cultivate it. Here's how: Make time to study for **the significance of creativity in** the study. Start by reading something every day. It doesn't matter if it's fiction, non-fiction or poetry. The point is to read regularly. If you want to cultivate creativity, you need to study regularly.

Creativity in the study is something that most people would agree to be valuable in life. Because we all know that creative people can solve problems, come up with new ideas, and produce things of value. However, if creativity is not recognized as an asset, it will remain undervalued. This will ultimately lead to under-utilizing this powerful skill in our lives.

How to train your brain to memorize things quickly

Some of you may already be good at memorizing things. But many people need to **train their brains to memorize things**

quickly. Here's how to do it. Firstly, you need to find a place where you won't be distracted by anything. Secondly, you need to make sure the material you're memorizing is in some way related to the subject you're trying to memorize. And thirdly, you need to write down everything you can remember about what you're trying to memorize. That way, your brain will go through its normal process of consolidating new information into long-term memory.

The secret to memorizing things is to get them into your subconscious mind. When you think about a fact, idea, or concept, repeat it repeatedly in your head. This repetition causes the memory to "store" the information in your brain. After a while, you don't even have to think about it. Your subconscious mind takes care of it. And it will do the same for anything else you need to remember.

How to train your brain to keep memorized material for a long time

Many people have trouble memorizing material for more than 2 or 3 weeks. Why is that? It's because they don't train their brains to retain information. The key to success is to use your brain to store information. Not your heart. It's all about your brain. That's why you need to learn **how to train your brain to keep memorized material for a long time.** The brain can keep information for a long time if you practice regularly.

Here are some of the most important steps.

- Write down what you want to remember.
- Use images, diagrams and lists of numbers.
- Repeat the things you want to remember.

- Create mnemonic devices, such as acronyms.
- Make flashcards.
- Memorize a keyword, phrase or sentence.
- 7. Get the words into your head, so they become a part of your personality.
- 8. Use different sensory inputs, such as images, sounds and smells.
- 9. Use mnemonics to help you remember the information.

How To Develop Your Brain to Store Information and Use It Where Needed

Using it is the best way to retain your information and improve your memory. You need to train your brain to learn and remember information. For example, reading books, taking notes, practising quizzes, playing fun learning games, participating in arts and crafts, and reviewing the information as soon as you understand it. These are all great ways to stimulate your brain. Think about how you might apply the information to something you care about.

A new study has shown that if you want to improve your memory, don't study what you already know. Instead, study the way you think. Your brain learns differently depending on the area you want to focus on. So study the ways that are most effective for your brain. Learn about the different ways to improve your memory and thinking skills. You'll find out that learning to do the things you're good at is the best way to learn how to be good at those other things, too.

What are the best possible outcomes if we train our

brain to be functional in the study

For most of us, there's no point in training our brains to become functional. We need to become functional now. But we can get better outcomes if we train our brains to become functional during the study. This is called "functional training", which is highly effective.

Learning to study is the best thing you can do to improve your mental ability and overall thinking skills. Study techniques are not rocket science. They are not difficult. They are simple. And once you get the hang of them, you will see the benefits.

Beautiful Mind for Career

The Significance of Self-Worth Affirmation in Career

There is only one thing that will keep you going. One thing that will motivate you to get through the day. And that is self-worth affirmation. A sense of self-worth. And if you don't feel good about yourself, you won't have any motivation to accomplish anything. Career success is all about building self-worth, and if you don't feel good about yourself, no matter how successful you become, you're not going to succeed.

No matter what you do, it is important to believe in yourself. There's nothing worse than going through life thinking you're no good. No one wants to be around someone who doubts themselves all the time. And I'm telling you: Self-worth affirmation is the secret to any success in life. A positive affirmation is a great way to start feeling better about yourself again when working with a self-esteem problem.

Best tips to develop being fearless in your Career

- Fear is the most powerful force that holds us back from our dreams.
- Some people are afraid to fail. Some people are afraid to succeed. But no matter what you're afraid of, the reality is you can't avoid failure.
- And the good news is you don't have to suffer through failure alone.
- Many people will support you if you're brave enough to face your fears.
- Some people will encourage you.
- Some people will hold you up.
- And some people will help you succeed.
- You can't escape your fears, but you can learn to live with them. And that's what fearlessness is all about.
- You can’t let fear control you.
- It’s time to stop letting fear hold you back.
- The only way to change your life is to change yourself.
- The best way to learn about fear is to look at the lives of other brave people.
- You cannot control yourself in life. But you can control how you react to it.
- If you're afraid of failure, you'll fail. But if you face the fear head-on, you'll succeed.

How to get maximum advantage of being respectful in Career

Respect is a universal language. When you respect others, you treat them as if they were special, important, and deserving of your best efforts. When you don't respect others, they feel they are expendable, unimportant, and undeserving of your best efforts. So, when you respect people, you create a better relationship, environment, and experience for everyone involved. But I have more to share with you. It's always best to be polite. And respectful. Especially if you want to make money. In your Career. When you go into a meeting. Or talk to a superior. Or just when you're dealing with people.

This is about "how to get maximum advantage of being respectful in career". This means you should learn to be polite in all circumstances because the person who has the power over you is you! To have power in the workplace, you must control the situation by being respectful.

Being respectful means being appreciative and being appreciative means taking pride in your work. It means respecting your boss. It means getting along with others. Furthermore, it means doing what you are supposed to do. And it means accepting responsibility for what happens due to your actions.

Best Possible Outcomes If We Develop Self-Worth Affirmation in Career

When you believe in yourself, you'll succeed. When you think you're not good enough, you'll fail. The difference between self-worth and self-esteem is important. A sense of self-worth is based on what you can do. The opinions of others do not determine it. You may get a lot of positive feedback from others about your work. But if you don't feel good about your work, it doesn't matter. You won't get any better when you think you're not good enough.

You can get the most out of your Career if you focus on building your self-worth affirmation in your Career. When you build your self-worth affirmation in your Career, you will attract the kind of people who will support and enhance your growth in the workplace. You will feel valued and respected. You will feel successful and powerful.

Thinking Out of the Box for Success in Career

Being innovative or creative in life is very important. Similarly, thinking out of the box is important to be successful in a career. It stands for delivering unique thoughts or concepts for the sake of your professional career.

Here are some tips

for this purpose.

Innovation Matters a Lot:

Innovation in life means a lot, and it dramatically changes your career. You should be able to introduce new things and ideas to the rest of the world. Be a man of your small world and get habitual to making decisions yourself! Be careful in following others; rather, make other people around follow you and your set trends.

Some may ask what innovation is and its benefits for your career! Well, it means introducing things, unlike others. This skill or quality earns you much fame, progress, respect, and social uplift! The people who possess the quality of innovation are always in demand in respect of professional careers. This skill pushes you to do the assigned tasks in your style and colour. Therefore, being innovative is necessary to progress in a professional career.

Hope sustains life!

Hope and staying for hope are always significant in life and professional career. Always hope for the best and see things and life from your perspective. Nothing is unachievable in life, and you can go miles before you leave. Optimistic people around you surely carry something extraordinary. They don't consider themselves losers.

In addition to the above facts, a hopeful attitude carries immense importance in the case of career development and grooming. The things or tasks which are impossible and undoable from anybody else's side may be practicable from your side. These are the cases of capacities and potentials. Hopefulness is always helpful in producing excellent results in professional streamlining and career.

All great things take time!

Remember this admitted fact for the rest of your life! Sometimes you are in a great hurry to finish the tasks at the earliest, but you forget the playing principle. What is it? It shows confidence at all levels in life. It is all about displaying courage and patience. It is all about having consistency in your work progress. This ability makes you think and design projects in your way.

Having big dreams and plans is a powerful source of self-motivation for everyone. It pushes you gradually, and if you show steadiness, you are meant to get successful in your career. Your plans must be different from others, and respect them as well. Hoping for all the big plans to work overnight causes huge damage to your career and self-confidence. Always think differently to make a difference in the course of your career.

Skills are the essence of life!

Being creative and skilful earns you fame and progress in your professional career. These give you the strength to move forward in life, and you can put your life on track. Skills possessed by you might be different compared to others. This fantastic quality makes you a better and more successful person in life. You cannot get through if you have no skills and special points.

Great progress is when you learn from your life and disseminate it further. Your career is always in the hanging position without skills. These are must-have things in a professional career. Your respective skills make you think differently to get success in your career. If you possess specific skills in some selective subjects, you have the opportunity to get ahead.

Doing things from a different perspective.

Thinking out of the box is hugely significant in real-life matters. Doing different things according to your perspective is a mammoth example. You need to be focused and centred in terms of your activities or plans. It gives you piles of confidence and support from others. You need to develop or introduce your ideas and thoughts. It will enable you to get along with the scenario. It will earn many more for you!

Embracing challenges and tough situations

Now, this amazing quality must be ranked at a reasonable level. Remember, if you start doing so, you will feel special areas for your practice. Accepting challenging situations and circumstances make you an empowered person. It teaches you how to accept and embrace challenges.

Developing strong leadership qualities

If you successfully develop this amazing trait in yourself, you can easily come to the top. You are always badly in need of strong interpersonal skills and methods. You must keep this thing with you as it will make you a better person. Leadership qualities are much appreciated and loved in this society.

Conclusion

The whole discussion's sum and substance are that thinking out of the box is very important in career development. This great quality earns you success and fame in your professional career. You must start thinking out of the box to be successful and mature in your career.

The Importance of Taking Risks in Life in Career

We meet many ups and downs in our life. Most of the time, we have to take risks to come out of them. Here, this article discusses the importance of taking risks in life to have a wonderful career. Our professional career depends on how much straightforward and focused we are.

There are certain occasions when we have to make bold decisions to support and stabilise our careers. Apart from that, being professional, we need to take timely decisions to put off all unpleasant things. All business activities and careers hinge on taking risks in life.

Here is a list describing the importance of taking risks in life in a career.

Getting new experiences

The biggest benefit of taking risks in a career is meeting with newer and newer experiences. These experiences are an amazing asset for us and give us a push towards achieving our targets in life. This thing is obvious that if we do not leap into the practical field, we will not be able to know about specific requirements. Whatever the conditions or circumstances, we must interact with the world to smoothen our way.

Availability of new opportunities

Another advantage of taking risks in a career is having new and fresh opportunities for professional grooming. It lets us move forward in life. We can create new slots for us. We can develop good relationships with others without dislodging them from their positions. We can easily make plans for our professional development in our careers. None can raise objections against our plans. Without taking risks and stepping forward in life, we can't avail ourselves of new opportunities to improve our careers. We always need to go ahead.

Competitive environment

When we start talking to others about our rights or problems, a competitive environment comes into place. We need to be aware of our rights and privileges at the workplace. We must interact with others to get the confidence necessary for ultimate career success. It is quite hard to understand the situations around without being a part of a competitive environment. We can take the initiative and risk to develop a competitive environment for ourselves and others.

Future rewards

Remember one thing; if we take pains and take risks today, it will surely reward us in the coming part of our professional life. In other words, taking risks and making bold decisions about our careers today will benefit us tomorrow. No pains, no gains! If we remain sitting workless and don't shape a plan, it will damage our future life in some way or the other. Without active thinking, planning, and taking risks in life, we can never enjoy a booming career. Rewarding the future demands continuous work and a professional approach on our part.

Meeting professional requirements

We can easily come up with the needs or requirements of our professional careers if we learn to take risks in life. It is almost impossible to understand others around us if we don't make ourselves part of them. We need to mingle with the world to understand the situations of the professional career.

Learning leadership skills

It is one of the enormous benefits of taking risks in life career. We are always able to prevent submissive approaches in life. Being submissive and extra apologetic can never furnish success for us. We need to take risks to be productive and prominent, among others. If we want to surpass others in life, we must make bold decisions to take our careers to new levels. We become future leaders by taking risks in life in our careers. This makes us stronger and braver, which is a striking element of leadership. Leaders are always bold and risk-takers.

Getting rid of the comfort zone

Taking risks in a career always helps us eliminate our comfort zone and laziness. We discussed earlier that taking risks makes us brave and fighting people. This quality is essential in career development. It helps in coming out of the comfort zone, and we get habitual to working hard honestly. Therefore, we can't grow on the career path without taking risks in life.

Quick achievement of career goals

We have certain targets or goals relating to our careers. Achieving these career goals means we are going positively and can succeed in professional life. This quick achievement of goals and objectives can never be possible if we are not addicted to taking risks in life's careers. Our timely decisions and actions matter significantly in getting a flourishing career ahead. Simply, it eases our way to a successful career.

Conclusion

In short, life is all about taking risks and taking brave decisions. We can also take tough steps in our professional careers through brave decisions. Remember! They say, **" Fortune favours the brave."**. So, we need to learn to take and combat risks in life's career.

The Power of Decision Making

Here, in this article, you will read about the power of decision-making in every department of life. Decision-making has always been very significant and supportive in a man's life. It not only serves in general life but also in the professional one. It deeply impacts your overall performance in all walks of life. The power of decision-making guides you towards having a strong command over leadership skills. It always places you in a commanding position. All great men in history earned a big name due to their decision-making power.

Here, you will read a list that describes the power of decision-making in your life. It highlights the important points.

Self-confidence

The biggest advantage of decision-making centres around self-confidence. In other words, we can say that the biggest power of decision-making is getting self-confidence. We know well that timely decisions are always in an organisation's or entity's greatest interest. It enhances the overall performance and progress.

Having confidence in oneself is very important for professional grooming and development. A person capable of doing things on his own accord and thinks freely is a suitable guy for any organisation. He acts freely and independently. The quality of decision-making makes him a different person compared to others. He carries out different projects fearlessly and tries his best to generate perfect results.

Personal and professional development

Another advantage of decision-making skills revolves around immense professional development. It creates numerous occasions and opportunities for a person. Its effectiveness and influence away everywhere. According to some findings, decisions play a crucial role in our personal and professional development at all levels. It lets us create our place in society.

The power of decision-making never goes unrewarded. Its benefits are great in number. After we join our professional line, we need to retain our reputation or worth as able workers. We need to get ourselves admitted into the market. We have no chance of showing any signs of weakness and fear. At this point, our skill or talent for making excellent decisions comes into play. It eventually serves us from various perspectives.

A step towards having leadership skills

Great leadership qualities and skills are due to the talent for decision-making. All great leaders were amazing decision-makers. They were not in the habit of relying on the decisions or plans made by others. They were innovators and always did their best to put up brilliant outcomes. Their decisions changed the destinies of their countries and nations.

The power of decision-making shows when we see newer and newer figures around us. The power of decision-making takes us toward becoming a great leader. Its magic is observed everywhere. Our institutions must feel responsible in this regard. They must bring learners ahead to learn the art of leadership. Our teachers can enhance their decision-making ability. They need to bring themselves to the front.

Improvement in management skills

A great decision maker is always a good manager. It's only a good decision maker who can manage different tasks excellently at the same time. Such a person is the selection of any company. When he starts making bold decisions, he becomes the hot favourite of his audience and juniors. He becomes an improved manager for his working station.

Management is always helpful and important in carrying out all the work satisfactorily. Good management skills are hugely beneficial for the rest of the staff. It serves in numerous ways. The power of decision-making centres around the welfare and uplift of any organisation.

Decision-making is timesaving!

It is always right! With the help of decision-making skills, we can create a huge difference. We can save time. We can also give this benefit to others around. The timely decisions change our lives. They have a deep impact on our personalities. We can develop an ideal self-image in front of other people.

The person who is quite lazy in making decisions is always at a loss. He can't act freely. He is considered unable to change the destiny of his country and nation. He is unable to bring revolution to the history of his country.

Remember! Decision makers are history makers. They are always influential people and are important to their nation.

Conclusion

The sum and the substance of the whole discussion are that decision has a strong impact on others. It helps in recognising your goals. It helps in shaping the future of your generations to come. We can never negate the importance of decision-making skills in real life. It can help boost your confidence and self-esteem. Apart from that, the power of decision-making smoothens the way of progress. It improves your professional career.

Beautiful Mind in Dealing with Family

How To Become Mature When Dealing with Family Matters

How To Improve the Way You Handle Family Issues?

If you're trying to improve the way you handle family issues, you should know that many psychologists say that the key to success is the ability to express what you feel and to listen to others. Try to get in touch with your feelings. Your feelings are important. They provide the energy for all of your actions. They also give you information about what you are thinking. You learn to hear what others are saying by listening to your feelings. And by listening to others, you learn to see your emotions.

Your marriage, family, and relationships are all key elements in your life. And, if you want to be successful, healthy and happy, you need to pay attention to how you handle them. So, here are some simple steps to help you improve your ability to handle family issues: Ask your spouse what they think. And listen. Listen carefully to what they say. Then let them know you hear what they have to say. Don't interrupt. Then give your opinion but remember that they may be right. Then, when you disagree with their opinion, let them know why you think differently. After that, make a decision.

10 Ways to Have Better Relationships With Your Family Members

Relationships can get tricky. Everyone has problems in their family. Some are bigger than others. Sometimes you may find yourself in conflict with someone close to you. There may be times when you don't agree with something your family member has done. That's okay. Just make sure you find a way to deal with it. Here are some tips to help you stay positive and find ways to work things out.

There are lots of ways to have better relationships with your family members. Here are ten of them.

- Don't blame them for your mistakes.
- Don't argue with them in front of their friends or family.
- They don't need to be reminded of their failures.
- Don't ignore them when you see them.
- Don't be ashamed of them when they visit.
- Give them credit where credit is due.
- Be proud of their accomplishments and encourage them to do even better.
- Do not expect them to read your mind.
- You should always remember that your family members are as important to you as they are to you.
- You should always remember that your family members are why you exist.

This is the stuff that works. No matter what you've been doing before, if you want to improve your relationships with your family members, You want to stop talking approximately yourself and start speaking about them!

How To Get Rid of The Fear And Anxiety Around Family Matters

The main fear for most families is what will happen if one parent dies or if they divorce. You may also wonder how you'll cope if you lose your job or if you get sick and can't work. These fears can cause stress in the family. Sometimes the way to deal with these fears is to look at things differently. Instead of what might happen, focus on what you can control. For example, if you're afraid that something bad will happen if your partner gets divorced, think about all the positive things that will happen instead of thinking about the worst thing. That's a much healthier perspective.

If you fear your family, you've got to find the courage to face it head-on. You need to find the right people to help you eliminate the fear. You need to have faith in yourself. And then you need to have faith in them. They're not perfect, but they love you just the same. They'll forgive your flaws as long as you forgive theirs. And then you'll learn what you need to do to eliminate the fear and maybe even the anxiety.

When it comes to family matters, many people feel fearful and anxious about the future. They worry about money, their parents' health, their children's education, etc. It's normal to feel concerned about these things. But that doesn't mean you have to live in fear and anxiety.

How to handle a family member that is constantly

making you mad

This is a tough one. But it's essential to maintain the right perspective. We can't all be successful in our careers. Or be loving, happy parents. Some of us may feel stuck in a job we don't like. Some of us may have trouble finding that special person to share our lives with. And some of us may feel burdened by the mistakes of our past. But that doesn't mean we have no choice. It just means that we must choose to look for the silver lining. Because life isn't fair, but it's also not hopeless. There are things we can do about it.

Many people find themselves in situations where they don't have a choice but to deal with a difficult family member. No one likes dealing with a difficult person. They don't like hearing their relatives complain. They don't like hearing their relatives insult them. Furthermore, they don't like having to act tough. And they don't like dealing with an unpleasant situation that seems to have no end.

When things are really tough, it can be tempting to vent anger. But if you feel like you're just getting nowhere, and talking about what's bothering you isn't helping, try this instead. Find someone you trust and talk to them. Talk to them about your family member and see if you can devise an action plan.

Conclusion

You must be careful how you react when dealing with your family. You must learn how to show patience, compassion, forgiveness, and understanding. And you must be willing to let go of those things you can't control. If you do these things, you will soon see a big difference in how you feel about yourself. And your family will also notice this difference.

How to Behave Good When Dealing with Family

The Secret of the Successful Relationship with Family

The secret to being happy in a relationship with your family is to accept yourself as you are. That way, you won't resent them for being what they are. They'll love you for who you are. And you'll enjoy having them as part of your life.

The secret of a successful relationship with family is to keep your eyes on the prize. When you start thinking about a relationship in terms of what you want from it, the relationship is in trouble. In the end, you will always get what you want. But when you think of your relationship in terms of the needs of your loved one, you'll find that you will enjoy the relationship a lot more. This will also give you the strength and confidence you need to stick to the relationship no matter what.

For years, psychologists and experts have studied relationships in families. They've concluded that the key to successful relationships is communication. The secret to communicating effectively is to understand each other. This way, you'll know what's happening inside someone's head and heart.

What You Should Know Before Dealing with Family

Your family is probably the most important person in your life. After all, they've been there when nothing else mattered. They've been there for you when everything else mattered. And they will be there for you when you have a problem. So, it's significant that you understand your family before dealing with them.

Everyone in your family wants you to be happy. No matter what they think. They may say they don't care about your happiness. They may say they don't mind if you don't talk to them. Or they may just be afraid to get involved. But they are just as you do.

It's never too late to repair family relationships. You can heal your relationship with your parents, siblings, in-laws, and even your partner if you let go of past hurts and forgive them. And it's possible to rebuild trust in any relationship.

How You Can Maintain a Strong Relationship with Your Family

There is no relationship more significant than the one with your family. A good relationship with your family can be one of the most fulfilling things in your life.

Here are some tips on how to maintain a strong relationship with your family:

- Learn to respect your family's point of view even if you disagree with it.
- Respect your family's feelings. If they are sad about something, try to understand why.
- Do your best to understand them, even if they don't understand you.

- Do your best to listen to their problems.
- Be there when they need you.
- Give them space.
- Remember that you only get one family.
- A strong relationship with your family will be one of the most valuable possessions you ever own. So make sure you know how to maintain it.
- One thing that can easily destroy a relationship with your family is fighting over money.
- You must agree on financial goals.
- Be willing to compromise and accept that your family may have different views.
- When you find common ground, you'll enjoy life together.

How to Treat Family Like You Would Want to Be Treated

Everyone should think about this: Why should you treat family like they deserve to be treated? The answer is simple: because they are family! You want your mother to feel like you care about her feelings. And you don't want to hurt your father's feelings by telling him something he doesn't want to hear. In fact, why would you ever want to hurt his feelings? The answer is that we need to treat people the way we want. That's the only way you'll live up to your standards.

This is the most important thing you can teach your kids: to treat people the way they want. Your kids must learn this lesson early in life. The sooner they learn this, the better. And the more they practice it, the stronger they'll become.

Conclusion

There's no way to live a happy life without dealing with family issues. But that doesn't mean you have to deal with them poorly. Here's how: First, try to be honest. Honesty is what makes it easier for others to forgive us. And second, remember to be compassionate. Compassion is what lets others see our good side.

How To Become Social Intelligent

What Makes a Person Social Intelligent

People with social intelligence tend to be happier, healthier, and more successful in life. They also seem to get along better with others. This is simple: they have developed good judgment and self-control. They use their judgment to make decisions. And they exercise self-control to keep their decisions from causing harm to themselves and others.

What makes a person socially intelligent? You'll probably get a thousand different answers if you ask a thousand people that question. But one of the best things you can do to become more socially intelligent is to start making social connections with people. That's it! That's all there is to it.

Socially intelligent people understand themselves, their relationships, and others to interact with their family and friends effectively. It takes self-knowledge, empathy, and self-control. To be socially intelligent, one must be able to recognize others' feelings, emotions, and needs. So how can we improve our skills in this area? We need to be aware of what makes us tick. That is the first step in communicating with those around us.

What Does It Mean To Be Social Intelligent

It's when you recognize the importance of socializing with people outside your immediate family. And when you learn how to be smart about it. It means you make time for people you care about. Furthermore, it means you choose your friends wisely. It means you keep in touch with people who've crossed your path. And you're willing to ask for help when you require it. Social intelligence means getting along with people. And making everyone feel good about themselves.

When we think about being socially intelligent, we often associate it with social networking. We think about our friend list. Our "friends" on Facebook. Our Twitter followers. We think about the numbers. But there is much more to it than just that. Being social intelligent includes your ability to: be a good listener. Remember and follow up with people. Be proactive. Be friendly. And be a good neighbour. Be polite. Be helpful. And be respectful.

10 Rules to Become Social Intelligent

Social intelligence is the ability to interact with people in social situations. It means being able to communicate with others effectively and effectively lead meetings and teams. It also means having the courage to speak up when you think things are wrong and having the courage to listen when others feel misunderstood.

Do you ever wonder how your friends always know what's happening in your life? Or what is your boss thinking? How do they always know exactly what's important to you? Here's your answer. They're just socially intelligent. And there are ten simple rules to follow to become social intelligent:

1) Take the time to listen,
2) Talk about yourself only when asked,
3) Keep your conversations short and relevant,
4) Never criticize others,
5) Be aware of body language,
6) Always maintain eye contact,
7) Look your conversation partner in the eye,
8) Speak slowly and clearly,
9) Let people finish their sentences,
10) Always maintain clarity

Social Intelligence allows people to be more aware of others and their needs. These ten rules should be the first step to becoming more socially intelligent.

The Power of Social Intelligence

Did you know that social intelligence has become the most important skill of the twenty-first century? When you master social intelligence, you can solve virtually any problem in your life because you can read others and their emotions and understand their motives. You will be able to control your emotions, actions, and speech. You can influence other people and get them to do what you want. Furthermore, you will be able to use the power of social intelligence to build successful relationships and make your dreams come true.

You require social intelligence if you want to increase your personal power, business power, and influence. You need to learn how to recognize, understand, and capitalize on the patterns and emotions of your network. You'll be amazed at the difference it makes in your life if you learn to put yourself in others' shoes. Social intelligence helps you see what someone else sees, feel what they feel and understand their point of view.

Conclusion

To become a socially intelligent person, you need to become more aware. More conscious. More alert. And most importantly, you are more interested in the world around you. And in the people in it. It may sound easy. But it's not. It's the hardest thing you'll ever learn. The hardest thing any of us will ever learn. Because being social intelligent doesn't come from books or seminars. It comes from experience.

Beautiful Mind in Life

The Art of Happiness

The art of happiness is of great importance in our life. It is always helpful in leading a perfect and balanced life. It plays a very significant role in our social development and overall performance in every walk of life. Happiness is the formula for a healthy and wealthy life. It leads to good outcomes and brings positive things to us in life.

Here we go to discuss the art of happiness and its importance. We will discuss its main points and striking features in building our ideal sketch of life.

The production of positive thoughts

The production of positive thoughts and ideas about life development generate from happiness and a sound mind. Gloominess and dissatisfaction are the main reasons behind the poor show in life. All the people who master the art of happiness lead a well-balanced and satisfying life.

Moreover, when competing with others, we can overcome fears

of lagging in life. For a successful life, developing strong habits is very important. Such positive habits put us on the way to progress and a life full of happiness. Therefore, to produce positive thinking, we need to stay happy and pleasing all the time. It's a great skill for our moving forward.

Self-confidence and satisfaction

Self-confidence and self-satisfaction are two main elements of our balanced life. We can never get them closer to us without taking the path of happiness. When we learn to be focused and happy all our life, we get the actual purpose of life. That is the essential thing to understand.

Happiness teaches us some precious lessons about a progressed life. We need to be humble and receptive in this regard. Dejectedness takes many things away from our lives, but happiness fills it with self-confidence and satisfaction. These two mutually combine to give a definitive shape to our lives.

Happiness- A source to win the people

The art of happiness is a powerful source of adorning our personalities. It is also a beneficial medium to win the hearts of the people around us. It makes them think positively about us. They do respect us by all means. This quality of ours makes us stronger and more popular among them.

Happiness fabricates a positive image of us in society. We receive a response that is acceptable and appreciative of us and strengthens our identity. This amazing thing pushes us forward to make a stunning development in society.

Mental peace and health

Another one on the list and very significant too carries benefits.

The huge favour and rewards we receive are mental peace and mental health. These two are much important in life. These are purely considered to be vital for our lives. The big magic of happiness centres around getting mental peace and health.

The art of happiness teaches us the science of staying on track with a healthy lifestyle. It takes us to the world of mental peace and health. Life cannot be ideal and performing for us without these two things.

Doing good to others.

"Do good, have good." This saying probably stands in place of goodness out of happiness. It won't be wrong to say that this thing is obvious and automatically working. Happiness is at a peak level when we start doing small tasks independently. Piles of happiness are there when you do good to others. The art of happiness makes us stronger and braver in our lives. It teaches us the lesson that sharing is always caring.

Making small gestures has a great charm and magic. Whenever we do good to others, we get pleasing outcomes in return. That's the absolute equation of life.

Happiness- A continuous process

The process of happiness is never-ending. It goes to ages ahead. It helps us in tracking the best tips for a good life. It is not just for a limited period; it remains the same. It gives us beneficial rewards in future as well. We cannot understand its magical powers. Happiness is for long periods.

A happy lifestyle changes our way of living. It also relates to our inner peace and satisfaction. It helps in shaping up our forthcoming future.

Fulfilling promises and meeting commitments

The greatest magic of the art of happiness revolves around fulfilling commitments. The art of happiness is that we sense our liabilities and responsibilities perfectly. We never try to bring a bad name to our personalities. Happiness teaches us to keep promises and meet commitments in our social life.

We learn to be productive and prominent. We also learn to earn respect, which is very important. These qualities show that we are happy and love meeting requirements and commitments.

So, to sum up, the whole discussion, the art of happiness proves very important and beneficial in the development of our personalities. This art joins people together. Happiness is the essence of life.

Positive Thinking in Life

Positive thinking plays a big role in our life. Positive thinking in life is of great significance. It is always helpful in generating desired results. Positive thoughts always push us towards doing more hard work to achieve our targets in life. It is a powerful source of personality development and self-motivation.

Positive thinking gives us enlightenment to know the real purpose of the struggles in life. It never gets faded, whatever the circumstances are.

Here are some main points!

High spirits

When we live our lives following the set principles of nature, we are bound to get ideal results. Our spirits are always high, and we don't want to look at the darker side of life. We feel like having a strong will. We believe in our struggles and never let ourselves drift away from the right path.

When we think positively that everything will take place the way we plan, then everything is good for us. Such good happenings result from positive thinking and staying optimistic about good actions.

A recipe for success

Success demands some specific things from the doers. Have we ever thought about these necessary things? Well, only a few of us try to come up with those things. Similarly, positively thinking about different matters is one of them. They say that positive thinking is a recipe for success and a must-have thing.

Positive thoughts always prove effective and work in the matter of getting successful in life. It won't be wrong to say that having a positive attitude and thinking is compulsory for ultimate success.

Stress management

Positive thinking has a great role in combating stress and anxiety. Positive thoughts always stay in action against the threat of stress and anxiety. When we shift our priorities and way of living and thinking about the world, our problems or issues decrease with every passing day. These disorders or problems strongly connect with our minds' plight and status. Keeping it engaged in good, positive activities and thoughts will save it from stress and other disorders.

Maintaining an optimistic attitude.

Here is another one on the list and much more important too. A positive attitude is not so tough, but maintaining the same is a big challenge for us. It is always the matter in some other things as well. So, starting it is not difficult but getting on with it is quite hard.

Staying optimistic about everything matters a lot. It is just a case of looking into the future. Maintaining or adopting an optimistic attitude is very important for all of us. It makes us think good things. Optimism and hard works are the essence of a common man's life and struggle. Maintaining the same is much more necessary for the betterment of the country.

Self-confidence

This is another benefit of having a positive attitude and thinking. Our positive thinking stirs up and vibrates our career line. We need to make ourselves strongly attached to healthy activity. Now the only thing that matters is following our professional career and its requirements.

With the help of this type of positive thinking, we are safe from any mental illness. If there's any other issue belonging to the streak, we need to highlight it. Positive thoughts always generate good gestures and wishes. It's quite important to have confidence in ourselves.

Self-motivation

This is also another great factor affecting positive thinking all the time. If we are fully engaged in getting it, then it is good to assess its plight or latest status as well. Positive thoughts always generate good gestures for us. This positive thinking gives us inspiration and self-motivation at all levels. Motivation is one of the signs of getting a changed mind and behaviour.

A change in lifestyle

It is very significant in this case. Having a good life is the dream of every one of us. But, getting it done in a real sense is the best thing. We must bring a good, pleasing change in lifestyle. If there is clear proof, then we should come over with a strong response. Our professional approach and positive thinking give us a clear shift and change in our lifestyle.

Self-satisfaction

Our way of conversing and dealing with others gives us a sense of self-satisfaction. With this approach, we stay optimistic about our struggles. This quality of satisfaction gives us an amazing feeling of enjoying inner peace. If we have negative thinking, we can't meet this happiness. Therefore, only positive thinking gets us piles of confidence and satisfaction.

Conclusion

Finally, the sum and the substance of the whole discussion depend on how to develop positive thinking in daily life matters. The element of positivity is of huge importance for us all. The magic of positive thinking makes us stronger and braver than ever before.

How-to Live-in Peace even in Harsh Circumstances

Our life is full of hardships, challenges, and tough situations. Here, this article will discuss how-to live-in peace even in harsh circumstances. It is always a test of our patience and persistence to tolerate the unwanted and unpleasant things in life. We have to take positive steps to combat such harsh circumstances in life. Without leaving these situations aside, we cannot have an ideal living and can't live in peace as well.

Let's discuss the essentials of living in peace in harsh circumstances. We will also discuss how to develop these qualities in ourselves.

Taking life from a lighter perspective

Taking life from a lighter perspective is very beneficial in staying calm and peaceful in tough situations. It is highly effective for fighting such circumstances. We need to know that all things happen under certain conditions, but after all, these have got proper solutions.

All circumstances never linger for long and are bound to end at a certain time in life. Therefore, we should never lose heart to seeing worse situations in life. We need to find ways to get rid of them successfully. We should always take the bull by the horns and try to understand the reality of life. We need to avoid stuffing our minds with useless things.

Thinking positively and staying optimistic

There is a famous saying that hope sustains life. It means that every good thing is possible in life, sticking to the power of positive thinking and an optimistic approach. When we think positively, we feel connected strongly with our goals. This is due to the magic of positivity and self-belief.

Positive thinking impacts our professional life too. Being positive and optimistic get together to end harsh circumstances in life. Positivity is always a great teacher for us. It teaches us how to come out of difficult times and react accordingly.

Putting harsh circumstances aside

It is admitted that worries get heavy on us if we consider them worth it. We should keep harsh circumstances at arm's length by not valuing them. If we succeed in achieving this thing, we will find some amazing changes in ourselves. There will be several solutions to the problems.

Putting tough situations off is also important as these help our overall development as good human beings. We will realize that life is not as hard to live as we think. It is all about living peacefully and with good resistance.

Adopting healthy and constructive activities

This is very important for remaining peaceful and calm in stressful situations. We must sense that all problems are due to careless actions on our side. We need to remain careful in making so many mistakes in our life. Anyhow, we should take to some good activities. These activities must be healthy and constructive for our overall development.

We can play some good games that make us happy and excited. We can get to the games like cricket, football, chess, snooker, and others. Apart from playing sports, we can get to the activities like speeches, writing, and reading different stuff from different authors.

Socializing

Socializing makes us friendly and cooperative with our fellow beings. If we think from a perspective, this is the actual purpose of our being in this world. We need to be humble and kind to others around us. This thing keeps us strong and inwardly satisfied and contented.

Meeting different people, particularly the best and close ones, keeps us free of worries. We forget about our issues and problems through their smiles and laughter. This thing has healing power. It has magical effects on our stressful life.

Avoid multitasking

Doing more than one work or task negatively impacts our overall social and domestic life. This activity is called multitasking. We should always avoid multitasking as it puts us into huge problems. We cannot keep focused on our special works or relationship with others.

We have always observed that we lose the whole game whenever we lose focus. So, to have good coordination and focus, we need to do only one task simultaneously. It will also enhance our performance.

Avoid over expectation

Remember! Expecting too much always hurts us in the end. Resultantly, this embarrassing situation saddens us. We fail to live successfully and peacefully. If we say that our mental peace and self-satisfaction are in our own hands, it won't be wrong to say so. So, always expect less and work harder.

Conclusion

The whole discussion's sum and substance are that we must interact with others. We need to be socially active and motivated. Remember, our faults and mistakes put us in trouble. We need to be focused. We need to retain the best things for our general well-being.

ABOUT THE AUTHOR

Muhammad Abdal is teacher of English and Arabic languages for beginners in Pakistan and multilingual article writer. Muhammad completed his master's degree in English Literature in the year 2021. Moreover, Muhammad is a well-known Arabic, Urdu and English translator for a private organisation. After experiencing speech disorder called "stuttering" and metal weakness because of speech disorder, Muhammad is now one of the best teachers who work on student's skill development and confidence building.

www.ingramcontent.com/pod-product-compliance
Lightning Source LLC
LaVergne TN
LVHW040957150826
845672LV00002B/734

* 9 7 9 8 8 4 8 4 0 2 2 4 7 *